by Daphne Greaves
illustrated by Jessica Wolk-Stanley

SCHOOL PUBLISHERS

Requests for permission to make copies of any part of the work should be addressed to School Permissions and Copyrights, Harcourt, Inc., 6277 Sea Harbor Drive, Orlando, Florida 32887-6777. Fax: 407-345-2418.

HARCOURT and the Harcourt Logo are trademarks of Harcourt, Inc., registered in the United States of America and/or other jurisdictions.

Printed in China

ISBN 10: 0-15-351510-4
ISBN 13: 978-0-15-351510-1

Ordering Options
ISBN 10: 0-15-351213-X (Grade 3 Advanced Collection)
ISBN 13: 978-0-15-351213-1 (Grade 3 Advanced Collection)
ISBN 10: 0-15-358100-X (package of 5)
ISBN 13: 978-0-15-358100-7 (package of 5)

4 5 6 7 8 9 10 985 12 11 10 09 08

Characters

Narrator 1	Jill	Cheri	Man 1
Narrator 2	Mom	Paul	Man 2
	Dad	Frufee	

Setting: Outside the Anywhere Anytime Travel Agency

Narrator 1: The Gold family has just pulled up in their brand new 3535 Sunstream.

Narrator 2: What a great looking car. It's a classic.

Narrator 1: Yes, it was invented around 2025. That was when oil was scarce. The Sunstream was the first car totally powered by the sun.

Narrator 2: So, where are the Golds going?

Narrator 1: They're headed to the Anywhere Anytime Travel Agency to plan their family vacation. They're just about to talk to travel agent Jill Chang.

Jill: Welcome! Please have a seat everyone.

Mom: Thank you. We're looking forward to planning our trip. I think we could all use a change of pace.

Jill: Well, if that's the case, how does two weeks in Frufee sound?

Mom: Where's that?

Jill: It's a planet in the Blue Galaxy.

Dad: I think I read an article about it in the travel section.

Cheri: What's it like there?

Jill: Incredible! The air tastes like chocolate.

Paul: I like that!

Dad: So long as it's not fattening.

Jill: I spent a week there last year, and to my amazement, I actually lost weight.

Mom: What are the Frufees like?

Jill: The inhabitants of Frufee are known for their strong emotions. They are very friendly and love tourists.

Cheri: Is that a picture of some Frufees in that poster?

Jill: Actually, that's just one Frufee.

Paul: Wow, two heads and ten hands!

Jill: Aren't they cute? Let's step into the travel room. I'll give you a five-minute tour of life on Frufee.

5

Narrator 2: We better explain what a travel room is for anyone still living in the past.

Narrator 1: Good idea. In the year 3535 travel agents can send tourists anywhere in the universe. People step into a functional travel room and take five-minute trips.

Narrator 2: It helps them decide where they want to spend their vacation.

Narrator 1: The Golds have just arrived in Frufee.

Paul: Wow, the air really does taste like chocolate.

Frufee: Hellooooo! Welcome to Frufee!

Dad: Hello, we're the Golds.

Frufee: Earthlings! I just LOVE Earthlings! Shake a hand, any hand!

Narrator 1: Frufees really like to shake hands.

Paul and Cheri: Hey! Ow!

Dad: That's quite a grip you've got there!

Frufee: Where are you staying?

Mom: We haven't decided yet.

Frufee: You must stay with me.

Dad: That's very nice of you, but—

Frufee: Really, it's no trouble. I have ample room for all of you. I don't live in a palace, but my home is very decent. Say you'll come, please!

Mom: Thanks. We'll think about it.

Frufee: I'm so excited! Group hug! Group huuuu— zzzz . . . zzzz . . .

Cheri: It looks like Frufee has fallen asleep.

Narrator 1: That's very typical. Frufee dozes all the time.

Narrator 2: What do you expect? All that emotion takes a lot of effort. Let's get back to the Golds at the travel agency.

Jill: So what did you think of Frufee?

Cheri: Well, it was very . . .

Paul: Interesting.

Mom: It's just that we were thinking maybe the trip should be educational.

Jill: That's a wonderful idea. How about a trip to colonial Williamsburg?

Mom: You mean the living history museum?

Cheri: Mom! Nobody goes there anymore.

Paul: Why go to a museum when you can see the real thing?

Jill: The kids are right. It's the latest thing in travel. We now have time machines, so you can vacation in ancient Egypt, the Roaring Twenties, or any time at all.

Mom: That's fantastic. Can we get a five-minute sample of colonial Williamsburg?

Jill: I'm sorry. Time travel is still too expensive for sample trips. However, we do have a special television that makes the past visible. Let's take a peek.

Man 1: The British are coming! Run! Run!

Dad: What's happening?

Jill: This is the year 1781. The British marched on Williamsburg that year.

Man 2: Liberty or death! Liberty or death!

Cheri: What is going on?

Dad: If I remember my American history correctly, the British took over Williamsburg in 1781.

Cheri: Look at all those people on horses. It's so exciting! Let's go there!

Paul: Can we? Can we?

Dad: Sorry, kids. That trip looks a little too dangerous.

Jill: If you like we could send you to a more peaceful time.

Mom: No, thank you, Jill. I think we'll stay in our own time.

Dad: I think that's best. We've all had so many responsibilities lately. It feels like we're permanently tired.

Jill: I know just how you feel. You want to relax. Last year, I was so tired the only place that beckoned to me was my bed.

Cheri: I'm not tired.

Paul: I don't want to go on vacation and sleep!

Jill: Of course you don't. I have the perfect vacation spot for the whole family.

Dad: Where?

Jill: Volcano Vacationland. It has pools surrounded by hot lava streams. It keeps the water nice and toasty.

Mom: That does sound relaxing.

Jill: I promise you'll never want to get out of the water.

Cheri: What else is there?

Jill: For kids, there's an amusement park. How would you like to ride on a wave of spurting molten lava?

Paul: That sounds great!

Dad: It's not dangerous?

Jill: Not at all. Scientists have found a way to completely control the volcano. Every night there's a lava show.

Jill: Best of all, Volcano Vacationland is right here on our planet. You can drive there.

Dad: Sign us up.

Jill: I'll book you a room with a view of the crater. The only thing required is a small deposit.

Mom: I wish we could go right now.

Paul: Yeah!

Cheri: Me, too!

Dad: Let's do it! Let's go right now.

Jill: Go ahead, you're all set. Have a wonderful time.

Narrator 2: Look at the Golds go! I didn't know the Sunstream could drive that fast! I guess they really need this vacation.

Narrator 1: Yeah, I bet they'll have a great time.

Narrator 2: I'm sure they will, but I really think they should have gone to Frufee!

Think Critically

1. Which vacation did Jill suggest to the Golds first?

2. Why did the Golds decide not to go to colonial Williamsburg?

3. What character traits do Frufees have?

4. How is the Gold family car different from cars today?

5. Which vacation would you have chosen for your family? Why?

 Science

Visit a Planet The Anywhere Anytime Travel Agency can send tourists anywhere in the universe. Find out about a planet in our solar system. Write a paragraph that describes what you would find on that planet if you visited it.

School-Home Connection Talk about vacations with a family member. Discuss what kinds of places each person would like to visit and why.

Word Count: 1,049